CLIMBING
POETREE

Naima Penniman

•

Alixa Garcia

Whit
Press

Seattle, Washington • Jackson Hole, Wyoming • www.WhitPress.org

Published by:

Whit Press
4701 SW Admiral Way, #125, Seattle, WA 98116
252 East Pearl, PO Box 13275, Jackson WY 83002
www.whitpress.org 206-295-1670

ISBN: 978-0-9836983-3-3

Library of Congress Control Number: 2013954254

First Edition: June 2014, Fourth Printing: March 2015

Design by: Tracy Lamb of Laughing Lamb Design, Jackson, Wyoming. Cover images from personal and image bank selections based on designs by Naima Penniman and Alixa Garcia of Climbing PoeTree.

Whit Press books are made possible in major part by . . .

the generous support of the following organizations and individuals: Margot Snowdon, Arianna Snowdon, Katie Nelson, Nassim Assefi, Lynn Garvey, Kerri Ballard & Bernadette Mansell, Connie Kemmerer, Emily Knobloch, Nell Fuqua, Janet Heron, Teresa Meadows, Kerry Lamb, David Adams & Cory Curtis, Laura & Ted Ladd, Francis Abbott, Hazel Singer, Kris & Tom Gridley, Connie Wieneke, Are Strom, Jeanne Ensign, our individual donors and the following organizations and businesses:

The Hill-Snowdon Foundation
Community Foundation of Jackson Hole
National Endowment for the Arts
Seattle Office of Arts & Cultural Affairs

To you all, our most heartfelt thanks and gratitude.

Printed in Canada

Naima Penniman

Alixa Garcia

CLIMBING
POETREE

Naima Penniman

Anonymous Was a Woman Who Wrote Poems

She had an appetite for starlight
under the billion watt blink
of a sleepless city
she could make out the silhouettes
of constellations
traced them behind her teeth
with her tongue
like how you spell a song
with just your body

"give me a reason for living"
she shouted at the sky
her own echo came back
a love song
that lullabied her into awakening
into her place in constellations
that hold up heaven
and inspire girls like her
to dance

despite and because of
the lovelessness
that built the buildings
that try to hide the dawning
she swore every star
had a sunrise

she walked through
the shadows
toward the promise of light
that kept her up at night
making love to her dreams

I can hear her footsteps
taking flight
the sound of the sun
breathing against midnight

here she comes again
I think we should
let her in

Being Human

I wonder if the sun debates dawn
some mornings
not wanting to rise
out of bed
from under the down-feather horizon

if the sky grows tired
of being everywhere at once
adapting to the mood
swings of the weather

if clouds drift off
trying to hold themselves together
make deals with gravity
to loiter a little longer

I wonder if rain is scared
of falling
if it has trouble
letting go

if snowflakes get sick
of being perfect all the time
each one
trying to be one-of-a-kind

I wonder if stars wish
upon themselves before they die
if they need to teach their young
how to shine

I wonder if shadows long
to just-for-once feel the sun
if they get lost in the shuffle
not knowing where they're from

I wonder if sunrise
and sunset
respect each other
even though they've never met

if volcanoes get stressed
if storms have regrets
if compost believes in life
after death

I wonder if breath ever thinks of suicide
if the wind just wants to sit
still sometimes
and watch the world pass by

if smoke was born
knowing how to rise
if rainbows get shy backstage
not sure if their colors match right

I wonder if lightning sets an alarm clock
to know when to crack
if rivers ever stop
and think of turning back

if streams meet the wrong sea
and their whole lives run off track
I wonder if the snow
wants to be black

if the soil thinks she's too dark
if butterflies want to cover up their marks
if rocks are self-conscious of their weight
if mountains are insecure of their strength

I wonder if waves get discouraged
crawling up the sand
only to be pulled back again
to where they began

if land feels stepped upon
if sand feels insignificant
if trees need to question their lovers
to know where they stand

if branches waver at the crossroads
unsure of which way to grow
if the leaves understand they're replaceable
and still dance when the wind blows

I wonder
where the moon goes
when she is in hiding
I want to find her there

and watch the ocean
spin from a distance
listen to her
stir in her sleep

effort give way to existence

Shipwreck

I wrote a poem one time
about my mother's manic-depressive suicidal tendencies
about how they locked her away
cause she overdosed
on her memories
and I read it

out loud to myself
and to my best friends
and a room full of strangers
and cried rainstorms

and it wasn't enough
to drown out the sirens
or to cover the shipwreck

at the bottom of her ocean

I inherited
when I was five
when she moved
to that far-away room
with padded edges
where they tore open our gifts
to inspect them each visit
and hid away what I had to give you
cause it could be fashioned into a weapon aimed inward
cause you were already that close to dead

that heart-shaped pendant
I bought you from K-mart
with the little fake rhinestones was
all that you needed
to puncture the balloon
that held captive
your last breath

and I thought it was
all that you needed
to remember:

I loved you
and your heart was beautiful
like the twinkling plastic rubies
I wanted you to wear everyday
like a prize
over that place that held the pain
the way I wore you
everyday, Mama

no, that poem
that rainstorm
wasn't enough
to flood the shipwreck
on the bottom

of your ocean

I swallowed
when I was twelve
and you weren't there
and the blood appeared
between my legs
so I started letting the men in
to stop the bleeding

cause I needed you
more than the drugs
I thought were the answers
to the problems
we couldn't talk about

no, that poem wasn't enough
that rain didn't cover the shipwreck
Granddaddy built in your womb
where I came from
we didn't talk about things like that
and I loved him
the way your tears ran in both directions at his funeral
the gravity of heaven and hell
the push and pull and thrust of
his weapon that didn't kill you
but left you dying

no, that rainstorm wasn't enough
to cover the shipwreck

at the bottom of your ocean

I colonized
and named after me
when I was nineteen
and stopped counting
the times you tried to kill yourself
stopped counting
the pills you hid in the sock drawer
when you came home
and told me in the eyes
I had all of them

it was my job
to make sure
you were taking
the right dose

not hoarding them
one by one
like bullets
for a shootout

you looked me
in the eyes
I stopped counting
and you lied
and I called 9-1-1
and the fire trucks came
in the driveway
to take you away

and I stopped counting
the times you said you loved me
cause it was not enough
to make you stay

no, that rain wasn't enough
to cover the shipwreck

in my ocean

the mast still sticks
its head above water
and I bump into it
not knowing
where it comes from

cause you're alive now
and you live in the woods
and read books
and knit things for your grandkids
and I love you

and I always
wanted that
to be enough
to keep you here
with us

running the surface of the world
bumping into things
and sinking
and rising
and sailing
sometimes

I think the storm is over
I watch you float now
with no lifeguard on duty
sometimes we won't talk for days
and I don't wake up in salt water
my heart hiding away in my throat

cause something saved you
all those times
shut off the bleeding
diluted the poison
you fed yourself, Mama

you are still here
Mama, Love
You. Are. Still. Here.

Black and White and Red All Over

like an old joke
everyone already knows
the punchline

Sled Road and Jackson Ave
do not intersect
but I was on the crossroads
with a go cart
made from scrap wood
I found out back by the shed

I am from dirt roads
and backstreet alleys
street-cart sugar slush
and wild blueberries

ponds and pavement
trailers and halfway houses
street lights and fireflies
crickets and car alarms

"Brownies aren't allowed in this school"
elementary
and playgrounds
where Snow White don't belong

apartheid in my lungs
segregated blood
every breath a traitor
our ancestors are at war
we are still settling up

what side are you on?
red rover, black paper

back against the fence

my face pressed against
the earth of my mother's breast
I saw the ocean
in my father's eyes

people thought he adopted us
asked what country we came from
in the checkout line

or that Mama was my Nanny
pushing me for pennies
in my stroller

I took turns
hating my self
disguising myself

baby powder and straightening irons
ebonics and black power

trying to fit in-
to a fraction

I am 50% white
and 70% water

like the earth

I am 50% black
and 70% water

like the world

and what color is blood?

and what color is breath?
and what color is God?

the color of water

Dew Drop

I was born premature
and grew up quick
learned to mother
my inner child
when I was just a kid

Mama, I needed you to live
like you needed me, to live
giving birth is like a life wish

an anchor to existence
a rope in the abyss
an umbilical chord cast down
the birth canal
the light at the end of the tunnel
the fire in my belly

Can you see me?

you gave me this light
do you remember?
you made me
in your image
strong like mountains

Can you put me back together?
when I fall apart
like dust
dissolving in the wind

Do you remember
how fragile
10 weeks premature born
torn from your womb
I raced to life

to interrupt your plot
for premature death

I am here
to catch your breath
when you fall
like oxygen
deflating from the body
or rise
like the slow leak
of a red balloon
headed toward the sun

Do you remember where you came from?

you are a dew drop
on a mountaintop's
open blossom
sourced from oceans

you have always been
whole, perfect and complete, Mama
Whole. Perfect. and Complete.

but you could never
complete me

when part of me was missing
locked away with you
behind security doors
and psych ward windows
like the plexiglass incubator
in the intensive care unit
where you'd wait
patiently for visiting hours
to bottle-feed my infancy

the way today
I wait for buses
and day passes
from mental health units
and your will to love
to align with your will
for life

and more importantly
your willingness to be loved
Mom, please
let. it. in.

I am overdosing for you
on copious amounts of affection
to make up for
what you are numb to
and desperate for

the heat of light to touch
your most tender places
the heart of yours
that does not stop beating
in time with mine

the heart of yours

that won't stop beating
even after
you thrust 91 pills down your throat
in hopes to never stop dreaming
fall asleep from this nightmare
be left alone with your demons

no matter how much
you give in to their shame
I will never stop believing

you are power.
you are source.
you are strength.

dew drop on an open blossom

Mama,
I believe in the blood
and milk you gave me
(spit out the poison, Mama)
in the truth of your love
that you mean it
enough to stay alive
(tell me the truth, Mama)

What are you thinking when you swallow?

Can you taste the aftermath
of your promises?
like pills linger
on your taste buds for days
death wishes congeal with i-love-yous
on your tongue
does it make you feel nauseous?
is it easier to fall asleep
than to awaken?

I was hallucinating
the last time you tried to commit
murder on my mother
I was swimming in your bright pink womb
sage smoke illuminating the rays of light
shooting through you
in the dark of the tunnel

I was praying for you
not because you need saving
but because you are my savior

and I saved you
a place in my heart
where no one else can fill

you cannot hide
truth is all there is

you are a dew drop
on a mountaintop's
open blossom
sourced from oceans

profound the depth
immense the strength
diamonds of sweat glisten
from the crest of waves
that never stop
dancing to the moon's music
never give up

no matter how many times
they return
to where they began

Something to Hold Onto

I want to give you
something to hold onto
so when my echo
disappears from your ears

you can still hear me
calling you
to the place we meet
in times like these

this is what makes me remember
why we all ended up here
bringing the things we came with
this is what gives me strength

to face myself
when I don't recognize you
to face you
when I don't recognize myself

beneath the dust I collect
when I stop walking
I will not stop
walking in your direction

there is
more
to life
than dying

cast a net toward the sunset
where the sea and sky
lay together like lovers
conceiving horizons

let the waves of your
surrender

crash against the shores
of inhibition

catch a star
plant it
deep inside
your soil

Precipitate

Imagine your life
were the sky
was the breath
you just took in

the sound waves
a tree makes
when it falls in the forest
and no one is looking

but you listened
to the sound
of its soul
escaping its body

concentric rings
mimic ripples
of rain drops
on water

our hearts infinite
like the oceans
parted ways
to make room for continents

so we'd have something
to stand on
as we rose
into our consciousness

the sky is
the limitless terrain
of the possible
possibly
loving you
is loving me

selfless
and self-fulfilling
like prophesy

•

Prophesy

the stars
have spent lifetimes
trying to reach us
with the message

our light
can inspire
solar systems
if we let it

shine
like the moon's reflection
of her suns
and daughters

great
great
grandmothers
and fathers

foretold this time
of great blessing
and slaughter
when we'd decide
between drought
and drowning in water

or rising
like mist
from rivers toxic
with dreams to be clouds
that give birth to rainwater

fall
pure to the earth
to quench this thirst
we'd forgotten
is the reason we struggle
in this web that we're caught in

not a trap
but an intricate pattern
a labyrinth
a snowflake
a crystal of water

or the rings of the tree
that still
makes a sound
long after it's fallen

in a forest that lived
even if no one saw it
and fed the world its breath
whether or not we applauded

one hand clapping
sounds a lot like
the rhythms we lost
in generations who sang
even as they departed

we paved concrete
over the pores of the earth
to make our lives harder
built buildings to scrape skies
trying to get closer to God
but moved farther

from the source
that birthed
the first light
in the darkness

we stole from our mother
and we continue to rob her
for diamonds and gold

and our ancestors' bones
disappeared from their coffins

turned hollow
so they could fly
despite the weight
of the fodder

before our feathers were trodden
and the dust
got us caught up
thinking pain is our fate

this
is what
we said
that we wanted

whether we knew it or not
the universe responded
to every vision and image
and nightmare we've thought of

our words are like bullets
and we call the shots
by their names
and they come running
with gifts in their pockets

impressions of
lessons of
the stories
life taught us

that our dreams
are impossible
so we keep them
in closets

now we stand
at the doorway
in the hallway
life brought us
to this cross roads
of lost hope
and undeniable promise

where we choose
between paths
beyond rightness
or wrongness
that will lead to the brink
of the planet's exhaustion

or the age of compassion
where the meek
become strongest
re-inherit
the earth
redefine progress

don't be scared of the spark
in the spell of great darkness

or afraid of the light
in the moment of dawning

or the heights you will reach
when you rise to your calling

release all your rain
call it flying
or falling

let go of your wanting
give in to your longing

live free of possessions
and full of belonging

to the intricate infiniteness
we're all a part of

the web
that you wove
in a dream
you'd forgotten

was the Creator
awakening
into your conscious

condensation of vapor
into a droplet
of water

Obituary for the Government, Eulogy for the Dead

Her name was Katrina
born of the waters
that swallowed middle passengers
who flew overboard
to save their grandkids
from what came after slavery

Her name was Katrina
born of the salt
of trails of tears
flooding stolen territory
generations of rivers
disappeared into the ocean

Her name was Katrina
born of the wind
that pushed rafts
from the yawning belly of Port-Au-Prince
to the fortress of Miami
gasping breath that lifted wings
across the deserts of Mexico
to unforgiving borders

Her name was Katrina
born of the heat
that cooked the world
the gaze of an ultraviolet sun
upon the violence of a nation
who thought God blessed only one

Her name was Katrina
she was born by the waters of Babylon
stirring in our sleep
with the force of breath
of every ancestor
whose blood
already stained our feet

and as the water splashed at her toes
Katrina's mother's water broke
flooded the sidewalks
with a puddle of the ocean

and as the water rose to her knees
the sky knelt in prayer
for strength to breathe
the horizon sunk below
the waters overflowing

and as the water crept up to her thighs
aircrafts descended from the skies
to take pictures of the sun setting
on the solitude of stranded families

and as the water rose to her womb
our daughters floated by in garbage cans
our sons swam against the current
of extinction

and as the water came to her chest
they separated the women from the men
shipped them to Auschwitz and Mississippi
the Super-dome, the dungeon in Cape Coast

and as the water rose to her chin
the television told stories
of looters and bandits
so a nation would fall back asleep
nodding their heads in disbelief
there was no one left
worth saving

and as the water came to her mouth
our screams were flooded
with all the blood that soaked the South
and all the pain
our grandfathers couldn't swallow

and as the water came to her nose
the stench of sewage and corpses
that already existed
rose to the surface
all the helicopters and soldiers
were in someone else's backyard
trampling someone else's sand castles

and as the water rose to her eyes
it dissolved the coating on the lies
there was no security
and this wasn't our
homeland

and as the water rose above her head
a thousand souls floated
from the bodies of the dead
their echoes turned
into the churning
of the ocean

Aftermath

When the waters calmed
like Noah's ark
there was no dove
no olive branch
just helicopters with cameras
and riot cops told to fire shots

this is occupied territory
like Palestine
Baghdad
or Watts

toxic water
guns were loaded
long before our dreams
were afterthoughts

in a man-made
nightmare
they tried to call
an act of God

there was no peace to keep
no security
no, this homeland
was never ours

in a state of emergency
instead of sending doctors
they declared a martial law

and the private mercenaries
that patrolled New Orleans
were the same stationed in Iraq
trained to fight terror
as if there were any terror
to combat
besides the terror
of being stranded
on a land that's sinking fast

where gunmen were told
to shoot the looters
as if there were any looting
half as bad
as the looting
of corporate merchants
with big government contracts

who profit off of suffering
as if suffering
were that
a profit margin drawn in Congress
back when the levees were intact

along those lines
the levees cracked
and the aftermath cast
eighteen hundred
loved ones dead

in condolence
Congressman Richard Baker
cleared his throat and said:
"We finally cleaned up
public housing in New Orleans.

We couldn't do it,
but God did!"

rid the city of the poor
rebuild the city for the rich
with contractors from everywhere
but New Orleans
coming in

folks in the projects
were forced to evacuate
even where Katrina didn't hit
then armed guards blocked the doorways
wouldn't let the residents back in

demolition scheduled
while people live in tents
under I-10

and thousands driven out the South
are still scattered across the States
with nothing to come home to
no means to return
all the tickets were one-way

eviction notice on the door
says you can't live here anymore
cause rent is late
FEMA owes child support
but told the courts
he no longer gonna pay

it's not hard to takeover a place
when its natives are displaced
New Orleans is being looted by profiteers
who wanna make over its face

plot to flood the lower ninth
to save the wealthier estates
as Mississippi renovates
with slot machines and condos
so you gotta win the lotto
if you plan to keep your place

it's the same
from gulf to gulf
the chip stackers
turn disaster
into profit
reaping billions
off the damage
that they started

in New Orleans, Port Au Prince, Iraq
paychecks from tax dollars
for no-bid contracts
so Halliburton
can rebuild the pillage
that they plotted

like Blackwater
the same military firm that massacred
17 Iraqis in a bloodbath
then in Katrina's aftermath
got paid to raid the streets
with fresh memories of Baghdad

The Gulf Coast is target practice
a dress rehearsal
for the New World Order
where money is worshiped
and culture's imported
on prayer beads
made in sweatshops
for Mardi Gras tourists

and did you hear the preacher-man say?
"New Orleans deserved to wash away
cause so many people there were gay!"

and if you read the founding statement
of the Salvation Army
they say they refuse to aid gays
now they've privatized God
and colonized our bodies
cause they got monopoly

on rescue
and salvation
and donations
from all of us

along with the Red Cross
who stole aid designated
for the Hurricane's daughters
used it to build new offices
on the island where 8 million live
surrounded by water

where Wall Street is God
and Giuliani gentrified Harlem
once the only place ex-slaves
could make art
so they rode the Apollo to stardom

till that space craft was hijacked
and hip hop, rock and jazz
became tools for the market
and now that it's cool to be black
whites wanna move back
to see what rose from the racism
their grandfathers pardoned

so now great grandsons of slaves
are displaced as Section 8
makes way for condos
and the homeless are jailed
so the sidewalks look polished
with the sweat of those who labored their lives
to fill the boss massa's wallet

Jim Crow's been abolished
but the government's lawless
across the nation since the eighties
housing departments demolished
78,000 project apartments
to fill "mixed-income" buildings
at least that's what they call it

from Chicago to Harlem
to the city that pre-Katrina
was three-quarters chocolate
block by block streets are bleached
so real estate sharks reap a profit
the flood just washed the skeletons
out of the closet

•

Aftershock

I was in India when I first learned of the magnitude 7.0 earthquake that decimated my grandfather's home-land. On the overnight train from Kerala to Goa, we were given a newspaper with morning tea. I hadn't seen any headlines since I left the U.S. "Dazed Haitians Dig for Survivors," was the bold header for the tiny article tucked in a tiny corner of the front page. As soon as its words came into my eyes, even before I understood what they meant, I was overtaken by a profound grief: deep, raw, and sudden. This poem, born from my sobbing, came out in one scribble, one breath. I dedicate it to the soul-survivors living and gone: a prayer for the graceful transition into ancestry for the fallen, for the safety and solace of the bereaved, and the inheritance of a saner, fairer, more just existence for the future generations of all Haitians.

I have not seen the pictures yet
of blood caked with ash
and anguished faces

photographs burned
into memory
stench carved
into day-mares

I have not glanced
the 2-D
broadcasts of desperation
thrust onto the screens
of our consciousness

but I can already see
the familiar forms
of vacant bodies
dim wet eyes
vision-stripped
futures vanished
stories re-scripted

I can already picture
the burnt girl child
scalding limbs flailing
in Vietnam's napalm blow

the woman's lifeless palms
turned skyward
on Tamil Nadu's shoreline
swept empty
by the tsunami's cesspool swallow

the wide-open scream
and unclosed hand
of the students fleeing
Soweto's school massacre
cradling their comrade's departed body

the corrals of runaway children
forced into soldiery
sleeping asylum in rows of hundreds
like factory-farmed fast-food flesh
or sardines
or slaves

the torsos of middle passage ships
the tattered surrender-flags
fanning 9th ward rooftops

the mass-graves of Auschwitz
the bombing of Gaza
9-11
and the 9-11 before that

and the countless
top-secret murders
of C.I.A. cointel
and S.O.A.-trained terrorists

I can picture
the sound of screams
that fall in a city
when no one is around
to hear it

the unfamiliar echoes
that escape the freshly-felled buildings
the last breaths wishing
upon the extinguished flames
of strewn street lamps

the homeless houses
the pathless roads

I can see the smells
putrefy the clouded air
the sweat of near-death
mingling with newly-crossed corpses
decaying in the chilling-heat
of an earth bombed with bricks

I can picture it

even though the Deccan Herald
had no space for a photo op
just a tiny front-page bottom-corner
one-column synopsis

and the AFP correspondent
forgot to sign his name
and de-membered
the memory
that all things are connected
to everything

his subtitle reads:
"Nature's Wrath"
and I laugh through my tears
at the thought of
Mama's Revenge

against a nation
that gave birth to itself
in shackles
and raised itself up
in shanties

refusing to surrender
to IMF debt measures
paybacks to French slave masters
rafts turned back to turbulent seas
and hurricanes near-lethal as Katrina
with less press than Britney

as if Mom
hasn't been force-fed crack
since 12 generations back
given asthma
from second-hand smog

and napalm-induced heart attacks

no wonder she's having
magnitude 7.0 epileptic seizures
in the most underdeveloped regions
of her body

mind tricked
into believing
like the rest of us
that the destiny of the poor
is more poverty
and bad things happen
to Black people

at least we learn
how to turn the lights out
when night falls
and how to sleep again
amidst the insomnia of insanity

may our rest
in peace-less-ness
inspire
awakening

today
humanity lost one to five
hundred thousand souls
between sunsets
grew twice as many wings
between dawns

our guardian angels are plotting
life after death
from the lunch counters of heaven

and hell will not survive
our minds' insistence
on some ending
different than this

and our fists clenched high
and our wrists rebuilding
and our palms wide open
to the phoenix
taking sprout
beneath the ash

They are Selling the Rain

they are selling the rain
they are leasing the rivers
they are auctioning off the oceans
to the highest bidders

as giant chunks of the polar ice caps
dislodge from the North Pole
and tourists flock to the site
to take pictures

there is disaster tourism
like there is disaster profiteering
off the torrential storms and the warring
and the wrath of global warming

who will get paid to rebuild?
and who will they build for?

who will endure the drought and the rain?
who will be safe and sound indoors?

who makes the missiles?
the smart bombs?
the rockets?

who gets raided?
and who gets paid
from whose pockets?

who gets sent off to war?
who dies
for whose profits?

who gets remembered?
who's been
forgotten?

•

Eye Contact

if we are
the truth we seek
let us speak
what we know to be

cause history is written by the victors
and news is broadcast by the captors
our desires are manufactured
and our self-image is back-lit
by the glow of the TV
and newspaper captions

our inner children been kidnapped
and are being held captive
in classrooms that teach us
that life's a transaction

nah, freedom ain't free!
when the ruling class
gets paid to be fascist

then say
you can purchase democracy
and we got equal access
to living in this building
whose foundation is cracking

cause the steeple was built in the basement
and the slave quarters
were fractions
of the whole picture
of an equation
whose math
was done backwards

then passed down
through teachings
that couldn't preach
what they practiced

so they use double speak
and keep us distracted
with addictions, strip malls
pop stars and fashion
and manufacture new gadgets
that make our eyes
avoid contact

cause if our third eyes align
as we look deeper
into each other's eyes
our higher selves
might recognize
that this is all a lie

Opulence

most people die
tryna get rich
not realizing the top slots
are already filled
by the founding fathers'
business partners'
right hand man
and grand kids
while there's
unquantifiable wealth
measured
in how much
we live

If We Can Wage War Overnight

what does it say about a city
that throws away
more than a whole nation consumes in a day?
from whom are we taking?
what is it that we waste?

what does it say about a nation
who spends half its yearly bread
on war and militia
what are we trying to defend?

what does it say about a government
who locks up a segment of its populace
then uses the profits to pay its debts?
who are we protecting?
what are we afraid of?

what's the meaning of the red in the flag?
and why were shades of brown the ones who bled?
to pave white stripes up to heaven
so false gods could snatch the stars
from overhead

who stole our wishes
and lit the match so we'd forget?
mesmerized by a fire
that's devouring our breath

there's an unnatural disaster
causing unnatural deaths
if there's enough food to feed the world
why is half the world still underfed?

if we can wage war overnight
why can't we know peace
lifetimes before we're dead?

if oil and forest are finite
just how much is left?
if we can manufacture mass destruction

why can't we make
creation last instead?

if the word of God rules this kingdom
just what is it that she said?
who are the disciples?
and who has been misled?

hold a mirror to your heart
what does it reflect?
what will be the message
of the legacy we've left?

What I Know

If I told you what I know
you would not believe me
so I will tell you
what I do not know

I do not know how bad it will get
before things get better

how many more
we will lose
to drought and flood
fire and famine

to mass incarceration
mass extinction
to hate crimes
and domestic violence
to the police
to TV
and toxic food

how many more we will lose
to pollution of our waterways
and air waves
and blood streams
our livers
and rivers and oceans
and imaginations

how many to the war on terror
and the war on drugs
and Crips and Bloods
and thugs and babies
and gays and immigrants
and indigenous people and differently-abled
and madly genius and schizophrenically gifted

and the war on thinking
and the war on love

how many more we will lose to the lust
for enough money to bribe God
to turn the other way

life is teetering on the precipice
of our willingness to let go
of what is killing us
and the earth's forgiveness
for what we have spoiled

regeneration is the natural order of existence
destiny will give birth to itself
re-spiraling the cycle
of the universe's chest rising
with each breath

will we be there to exhale?

Burn

Please do not fight my fire
let it burn
devour
the putrid remains
of what is left
of yesterday

your fire hoses
and attack dogs
keep them away
from our bodies
mr. officer

please don't arrest tomorrow
or the day after

we need them for our planting

in times of war
we save seeds
from the species
extinct from your blow

hide them
under our tongues
deep below the ground

harvest peace long after
the fragrance of her fruit
has been forgotten

and we will feed you
when you come to us
on your knees
weighed down from weaponry
begging forgiveness
and water

we will share our medicine
until you weep
at the resemblance
of our faces

you will remember our names
and your numbers
will crumble to dust
bankrupt

your blood money
will be as worthless
as your guns

Remember Me

I.

the brutal whisper of city wind
my back pressed against the buildings
waiting for new words to grow in my mouth
the desert of my barren tongue
no harvest for my hunger

my arms rust
and wilted
like the flowers
cornered in
shadows of property

I am surrounded
brick by brick
in the thick of my memory
abandoned like
a featherless child

I learned to scream before I talked
how to fly before I walked
my first step forgot
how to lift me past these rooftops
my breath lost in the wind

II.

the dead elevator would wait permanently
stay put
like the echoes of my mother's screaming
stay put
like the mattress I couldn't leave from

I was dreaming
playground games in shades of
bubble gum on pavement
black as angels

away from the bleeding air
that hung like exhaust in the kitchen
cold doorknobs that keep silent
like the graves of our Mothers

we're all waiting
for the red noise
to engulf us

III.

I stayed put for 18 years
before dragging myself through the streets at dawn
in search of bread and shoes
and something sacred

walking the thin line
where the sky meets the pavement
the edge of insanity and peace of mind

I surrender to shadows
no where left to hide

IV.

guilty of surviving in this face-lift city
the price of breathing went up
this metropolis could no longer afford my exhale
fingerprints, handcuffs
puddles in my footsteps

V.

this ain't no
flowers through concrete story
no silk over stone

lately I've grown accustomed to
spine on the floor
collecting salt in my hair

there's no sky behind bars
I can feel myself dying
the moon has lost its abundance

VI.

one day I woke up in prison
I was born here
I'm gon' die here

500 years without parole
our shapes molded
to the cages that held us

dream dust sifts between fingers
they're building walls
instead of bridges

God whispered my birth wish
I don't expect your laws
to justify me

VII.

I couldn't imagine days like these
throwing pebbles at the sunset
from behind the seventh wall

we're all
alone
in here

all two million of us
two million sad stories
miserable, repulsive

packed tight
like cargo
in the septic of middle-america

VIII.

I couldn't imagine days like these
up to my head and
down on my knees

gathering my promises
searching for something as certain
as the concrete against my palm

I am writing this poem to survive

IX.

promise me
remember me

like a flower bursting though concrete
like silk draped over stone

History Repeats

a civil war's been waged on drugs
to rid America of crime
but the criminals went building prisons
now their victims do the time

the system spreads the sickness
convicts the symptoms for existing
insisting streets are safe now
cause now we all in prison

just cause the KKK is cloaked
in blue instead of white
they still go killing brothers
every other night

just cause the lynching's legal
and executed by the state
they still obliterate our race
through blatant acts of hate

how much longer
we gonna have to wait?
I thought freedom was a'coming
we still ain't set a date

we're a billion dollars short
one-hundred-thousand
days too late
the population in prison's risen 8 times
what it was in nineteen '78

more brothers serve time behind bars
than those that graduate
and my sisters are filling prisons
at more than four times the rate

the poor are living behind bars
the wealthy behind gates
and the slums that house one thousand
are as big as one estate

Martin Jr. had a dream
that some day we'd relate
dreams now wait in picket lines
while the courts decide our fate

and George Jr.'s vision
mixed with capitalism
turned public policy
into the private prisons

the crime rate's lessened
while the inmates risen
the poor get locked up
the real thieves keep living

judges are taking
what God has given
wrote Elijah's life sentence
before he turned 27

and more innocent men
get shot by cops
than lost their lives
in 9-11

this land ain't your land
this land ain't mine
but the criminals who stole it
are getting tough on crime

the subliminal hypnosis
breeds neurosis in the mind
time could have served us good
instead we're serving time

an eye for an eye
till the whole world's blind

and we can't even picture it
something different than
the predicament
we're living in

a land where lynching's justified
by bible scriptures and

can I get a witness?

who put our ancestors up
for retail sale?
who's caging our youth
inside the jails?

history repeats
we still dying for a profit
who got this started?
and who's gonna stop this?

Blood on the Sheets

*For Shani Baraka and Rayshon Holmes (a.k.a.
Ray Ray, a.k.a. Isis), black lesbian lovers who
were gunned down in the home Shani shared
with her sister in Newark, 3 months after Sakia
Gunn's tragic murder*

Shani Baraka was killed
on my birthday

her mother's knees buckled
under the weight
of her feathers
falling like autumn

she clutched the warmth
of her hand
dissolving
as her body lay silent

Isis, you were
too much woman
for this world
too much man

for this world stole your breath away
punched holes in your dyke body
so they could see the light
come through

you were a constellation
of stars, Shani
too bright for this world
to see

the weight of your name
tattooed on your shoulders
we will not erase it, Isis
no shame, no silence

Shani, you don't need no
unconditional love
your loving is no condition
no symptom, no sickness

our love needs
no convincing
it comes easy
like your love, Shani

and Ray Ray,
come now to the place
where men are unafraid
of the love that is stronger
than their pain

an ocean of laughter
is waiting for you there
like a wide open lover

your lips
made of fire
will not quiet

Isis, your eyes too open
Shani, daughter of pistol
and poems that kill

your ashes will stick
to our memories
like the swollen face of Emmet Till
extinguished the last thread of doubt
God was waiting on us

the lunch counters and buses
will be filled with your dust, Shani
we will bring it there

scatter you across the ocean
while your soul
stirs thing up in heaven
'til the ghosts of one million angels
come stage sit ins
in the churches

we will wear your name
on our shoulders, Isis
bear your name on our foreheads, Shani
in between our teeth
until no one
is afraid to read it

and if the fire comes, Shani
we will feed it
with the timber you collected
to build your home
until the smoke sculpts itself
into your temple
no bullet or stone could enter

and there, my sisters
won't you go on loving
won't you go on loving
go on loving
won't you?!
go on
loving

Overcoming

this is the moment
when we gather up
our fallen angels
and build a temple
invincible

we've been hibernating below
the surface of the world
growing roots
dreaming of sun
thirsting for rain

we sprout
crack concrete
overcome
the bullets and toxic exhale
of a machine built to kill

we rise
like sunshine
the shadows, our memory
of the struggle it took
to lift our heads above drowning

we breathe
exhale this sky full of stars
pregnant with moon
trace the constellations
in the shape of
our revelation for tomorrow

this tomorrow has no name
but we are calling her forth
this tomorrow is not the same
as yesterday
but she is as ancient
as the world

we are ready for light
we are ready to live
ready to hold each other   .
against the rim of existence

cause they who build concrete
against the corners of our hearts
need to feel our resistance
like a million tender blades of grass
cracking sidewalks apart

reminding your runaway child
there is no place that love cannot find you

there is no place
that love cannot find you

there is
no place
that love cannot
find you

We Will Survive

We survived the fires
of Selma and Nagasaki
and we will survive Palestine

we survived Vietnam
and Wounded Knee
Rwanda and Mississippi

the fifty stripes
around our stars
fifty years to life
behind their bars

we survived middle school
and self-inflicted scars

pink triangles and Stonewall

losing our mothers
to our fathers' hands

we survived famine and genocide
came back from the dead
and spread like wildfire

we survived slavery
and gas chambers
biochemical warfare
and lynching

the seeds from our strange fruit
been sprinkled across this terrain
by our angels

and everywhere we land
we gonna take root

and every inch of rock
mud and sand
we gonna breakthrough

you're here right now
I'm seeing you
with my own two eyes

think of all the demons
that tried to take you
and you still survived

and
we
will
survive

the thickening water
and vanishing air
the electric chairs
and lethal injections
thefts and gold mines

we will survive the bullets
and coat hangers
strip searches
and fumigations
the embargoes
and bounties
and bombings

we will survive the factories
and hospital visits
the concrete
the police beatings
the cutbacks
the evictions
the droughts
the prisons

we will survive
the reincarnation of our souls
in our little cousin's eyes

I've lived a thousand lives
that's how I know

We. Will. Survive

If You Were You

If you were a cop
would you stop the hypocrisy?
turn your guns on the real criminals
strip search the colonists for stolen property

if you were a teacher
would you teach your students the truth?
make origami birds from the history books
fly back in time for the proof

if you were a newscaster
would you tear up the script?
on channel six live at prime time
tell shit like it is

if you were a soldier
would you dismantle the bombs?
hoard all the bullets under your cot
stuff those rifles with songs

if you were a warden
would you smuggle poems
in the bologna and cheese?
whisper the geometry of keys
in the captives ears when they sleep
so when they wake in the dawn
they'll know how to set themselves free

if you were a millionaire
would you douse your dollars in gasoline?
set them on fire on Wall Street
to quarantine this disease

if you were a doctor
would you sling rocks and sell trees?
hang out on the corner
pockets full of vaccines

if you were a carpenter
would you build a castle for every queen?
who collects bottles and cardboard
to build her nest on the street

if you were a mother
would you teach your kids to be proud?
of every drop of their blood, breath, and bodies
so they'd live life aloud

if you had a voice
would you speak up?

if you had eyes,
would you see us?

if you had feet
would you stand up?

if you had hands
would you lift up?

If you had nothing
would you still never give up?

if you were you
what would you do?

what would you do
if you were you?

Prerequisites for Preservation

we're gonna need to get organized
live beyond boundaries
soften our hearts
talk to each other

we're gonna need to leave behind our baggage
relinquish our comfort
release our control
coexist

we're gonna need to give up our addictions
confront our pain
ask for help
give more than we take

we're gonna need to dream bigger
work harder
get dirty
take time

we're gonna need to remember
we're gonna need to forgive
we're gonna need to let go
we're gonna need to let go

we're gonna need to feel fully
revive our intuition
make up our minds
enact change

we're gonna need to look at ourselves
reconcile our ignorance
sacrifice shame
make amends

we're gonna need to need less
peel away the nonessential
go hungry
break a sweat

we're gonna need to heal our fears
tell our secrets
share with our enemies
love ourselves

we're gonna need to study existence
refine our dreams
mediate our shadows
cure our disbelief

we're gonna need to practice magic
we're gonna need to cherish water
we're gonna need to grieve
we're gonna need to move on

we're gonna need to stay focused
we're gonna need to be strong
tend our commitment to beauty
fuel our devotion to truth

we're gonna need to pray
we're gonna need to follow through

endure burning
we're gonna need to

surrender
we're gonna need to trust

we're gonna need to give light
we're gonna give light
we are light
we are

●

Awaken

We are in the wake
of a great shifting

awaken

you better free your mind
before they illegalize thought

there's a war going on
the first casualty was truth
and it's inside you

the universe is counting on our belief
that faith
is more powerful than fear

and in that the shifting moment
we'll all remember
why we're here

in a world where you're assassinated
for having a dream
and the rich spend 9 billion a year
to control our ideas
and visions are televised
so things aren't what they seem

we gotta believe
in a world where
there's room enough for everyone
to breathe

cause reality is made up
of 7 billion thoughts
who made up their minds
of what's real and what's not

so I stopped believing
in false idols
of war, greed
and hate is not worth my faith

love is God

and God is truth
and truth is you
and you are me
and I am everything
and everything is nothing
and nothing is the birthplace of creation
and transformation is possible

and you are proof

we were born right now
for a reason
we can be whatever
we give ourselves the power to be

and right now we need

day dreamers
        gate keepers
                truth speakers
                        light bearers

bridge builders
        web weavers
                food growers
                        wound healers
trail blazers
        cage breakers
                life lovers
                        peace makers

give what you most
deeply desire
to give

every moment
you are choosing to live
or you are waiting

why would a flower
hesitate to open?

now is the only moment

rain drop
let go
become the ocean

possibility is
as wide as
the space
we create
to hold it

Possibility

you are that promise
let your rain fall down
everything you do right now
is your calling

come undone
under the weight of your breathing
that which can be taken away from you
is not worth keeping

let go of your gifts
that you may receive them
possibility is as wide
as our believing

This

let this be
the best day of your life
cause it's the one
you are living

let this moment
be a gift
cause it's what
you've been given

live as if this
were the end
cause it's just
the beginning

close your eyes
open wide
tell me
what is your vision?

Every Little Thing

if every little thing that you did
made a difference
would you do things
a little different?

if every thing that you said
built the world
would you be the sacred keeper
of your word?

would you believe me
if I told you
you're the reason
we are here?

would there be meaning
to your breathing
if your exhale
made the air?

Serving Life

my life sentence
is a question
the answer
is yes

Wanderer

wander this way
follow the trail of your thoughts
like a river stone skipping
across a still pond

or the ridges of records
scratching this song
turning tables like deejays
drummers sound out this call

of rebellion, abolition
the downfall of walls
the echo resounding
as each brick takes its fall

stacks into a pyramid
that kisses the stars
faith is a ladder
a thousand rungs tall

keep climbing skyward
till the ladder dissolves
then become still
with awe

wanderer,
I don't care what name
you choose to call up to God

if you spent your whole life
living in indecision
thus far

I'm looking at you now
I know who
you are

make contact
with your own eyes
then choose what you want

know it's coming
that's the act
of call and response

it's the law
golden rule
ask and attract what you want

the universe will respond
in the shape
of your thoughts

speak the truth
that you
have been dying to hear

cause the world is thirsty
and the message
is clear

as the water
that quenches
our deepest dark fears

of the shadows
cast from light
traveling thousands of years

Renewal

God,
let us fall in love
with ourselves once again

grateful for each breath
like it was our life's wish
an eyelash in the wind

crescent moon rising
like an angel
with embryonic wings

Eternal Spring

Euphoria is an arrival at truth
when you don't have to go anywhere

it goes with you
it becomes you

it does not balance
on the rim of circumstance

it is the eternal spring
within your being

The Vibration of God

You got me humming
and I like the vibration
I feel echoing beneath my skin

when my future remembers you
like flash backs
from past life prayers

it's deep
this water

your got me rising
and floating
and sinking like breath

your fingerprints
are showing up in places
you didn't touch me yet

I hear the rhythm
even in the still silence

even in the clash of overcrowded corners
I feel the pulse

even with my eyes closed
and volume down
and clothes off
and candle lit

I feel the vibration of God
reincarnated under an endless sky

we are making love beyond the body

Alive

I am certain I am alive
and I know I am dreaming

your face is a sunset
that doesn't leave me at night

your eyes a million candles
in an indigo sky

you remind me of the love
that inspired God to make sunlight

may I be the moon
calling back to you tonight?

glowing brighter than all the earth's electricity
from the reflection of your shine

undressed from the last thread of shadow
nothing left to hide

By Myself

I need
to fall in love
with myself
all by myself

not assemble pieces
of my reflection
in your, her eyes
and call it home

nestle there
in the company
of 1000 voices
that know my name

waiting for them
to tell me
what I already know
and need to find again

in the company
of my soul
naked and alone
and so, so full

●

I Am Here

I am here
as soon as you look for me
I will appear
in the same place
I always wait for you

where
fire and water
live together
inside you

where
your whisper and your screaming
sleep together
nestled in the echo
of your ocean

where
stones lose their gravity
and stars fall
faster than their light
speeds to touch you

where
laughter lingers
and tears collect
in puddles

where
love goes
in wartime

I am there

I always wait for you

where pain cannot hurt you
where ghosts bring their dead
where life is born again

I am there
holding your breath

in the ship bottom of your sorrow
in the tangle of your fury
the oven of your fear

I am there
cradling your palm
collecting your river water
counting your heart beat like gold

in the springtime of your passion
the rising of your courage
the waking of your dream
I am there

in the space between you
and your name
in deception's changing room
I am there naked

I always wait for you there

beneath you
there beside you
there behind you
there inside you

look me in the eyes
where only you can see
smile upon me

shine your light
in my throat

open your mouth to me
I promise

I am here

•

Alixa Garcia

•

Tightly Folded Forests

Books are tightly folded forests
whose branches once wrote a thousand stories

it's poetic

how we steal the earth's breath
to jot down memories

unearth the roots
for ghostly pages
to record perceived beliefs and reason
that bind and simultaneously change
like seasons

they say history is the greatest prophet
even when spelled poorly
at best a quivering knowledge
lacking proof
and all one sided

So I write on fallen carcasses
to tell the truth of stolen goddesses

she
who crossed borders
lost language and her moccasins
she
who scrubbed toilets
to pay for her son's coffin
she
who never made it out alive
her bedroom lined with caution tape
anonymous

I write on fallen carcasses
till her story makes history
and patriarchy's path
descends back to the valley

She atop the highest peak
remembering
sunlight stored in roots
gave us back the fire
and pulled us from the darkness

Before I Awoke

In the depth of darkness
I spun around the sun

I followed the beat of a heart
like dancers to drums
I caught spirit
in the womb

I named myself God
cause she was I
as I made my way into
flesh and bone
I grew no wings
so I borrowed song

I pushed
transforming her ribs so
I could grow

She let me

I had only a memory of this place
where land is shifted
and destroyed for gold

I shifted her hips
so I could grow

She let me

She was the breath
my lungs didn't know

She was the water
my body grew to resemble
but this drought in my throat
got me wondering
if she'll make it
past my ability to remember

First cries are premonitions
to life
before I woke up
I remembered

I was born of ions
nucleus and cellular
I was microcosmic and universal

I spun around the sun
in the depth of darkness
I followed the beat of a heart
like dancers to drums
I caught spirit
in her womb

The Journey

The journey at times
was insanely gory
but our resilience grows
like morning glories
bio remediation
to our souls' story

bottom of boats
in death's inventory
but we resurrect
like Lazarus

life is mandatory

She don't stop
and we don't quit
against death squads
we tightly knit
making soul bonds
in human links
until our fear subsides
and our sorrows sink

below the bottom-line of hell
where again you hear the angelic sing
aloud
from classrooms to protest lines

Our word is truth in a drilling bit
to hole punch their lies
and let light in

Our children smell glue
to feel full
but South America
Africa
India
you name it
we're rich

We're remembering
how to recommit
to life's sacred geometry

Against their silent murder
we be an orchestra pit

We're electrifying
this time we won't let you
touch the toggle switch
We are shape-shifters
dare to massacre this wish
Alchemists who know the truth
that too many truths have gone amiss

Your globalized agenda
might make some bewitched

but your sales pitch
no matter how glitterfied
starts feeling soon like a relentless itch
addicted to the scratching

but we're from outer space
immune, can't get what you're catching
and our spaceships
don't need building permits
we make music from star guitars*
speak in riddles to build this bridge
From Brooklyn to Eritrea
our moonlit dreaming drips
nectar from our souls
until this soil's enriched

Mr. CEO
We are the back up hard drive
to your humanity
we're storing memories you forgot
traded them in for a murderous plot

The forest of your imagination
you paved for a parking lot
to single file your strategies
but life
is a love knot

Your crimes against us
will get you a mug shot
permanently hung
in the security room of heaven
where angels surgically remove
spiritual blood clots

This ain't about religion
you converted that like missionaries
masking blind spots
white savior in our churches
but in the Bible
he's got a woolly top
The Creator's mad at you
for twisting up the plot
for profit selling prophets
Jesus, Buddha and Allah

Rumi, Hafiz, Sojourner
thank God never got caught
they taught me
how to kill the slave
inside the aching heart
turn truth to ammunition
and pain into this art

Footnote *Meklit Hadero (star guitar)

For the Woman Who Raised Me Right

I.

My abuelita collected sticks and stones
and broke her bones
to build fires
and cook sancocho for the men

by the age of ten
she was four years shy
of getting married off
to a man four times her age

Her womb would expand into the universe
she would bear 3 daughters and 2 sons
who would orbit around her
like planets to the sun
multiplied by galaxies
undone
like families to migration

That's how she lost even the youngest one
cause when you grow up
in the most violent country
this side of the Atlantic
there are risks involved
when bringing pure light
into the evening's tide

She's always been my brightest star
after her husband died
her second marriage
was to God

she built a castle
so rich inside her heart
that all the poverty that touched us
never touched us

She is a poet
whose prose
despite internalized hatred
undid racist booby trapped explosions
she taught us metaphor
like when they say
you're dirt poor
they mean
you're nutrient rich
everything you plant from without
grows from within

II.

If you cut the land in half
you will find the color of my abuelita
deep rich coffee plantations
where blood and bones
seeped into weathered earth
housed teeth and broken smiles
the ghost of feet surrendered
left hollow impressions

Aborted children
reincarnated
to seed a revolution
that started out promising
like their birth
until back door deals
with the First World
cut the umbilical cord
prematurely

casting a reflection as violent as them
now their revolt kidnaps babies
for a war with no end
the war on drugs
has always been
the malnourished child
obsessively fed
in the rolling hills of Fredonia, Mira Flores
the inner cities of Bogota and Medellin

It was there I was born
second generation to her childhood
where she walked an hour to school
bare-soles through dirt roads
4 times in one day
by the evening mathematics had no place in the kitchen
schooling was secondary
so when she graduated from college
the day I graduated from high school
in a country foreign to her
she became my superhero
who spoke broken English—
only when she had to

III.

My abuelita's spirit towers at 4 feet
11 inches to spare her reach
into the tender corners of heaven
the palms of her hands have A's instead of M's
for ángel
or angel
spelt the same
and you need them both
whichever way you wanna say
cause young men
strap AKs and chew coca leaves
where tourists think they can tell the difference
between thugs and the police

it wasn't always like this

IV.

First star wishes
cross the sky
like star-crossed lovers
and crossed-finger dreaming
can't undo the pain
of a collective memory
so traumatized

that my abuelita's placenta
like a tree rooted
hung ghostly nooses
'cause colonization white washed
her mother's moonless night skin
with self-loathing

Self-Love hung heavy
like a burned victim's memory
the family tree begged for saving

It wasn't always like this

V.

DNA strands carry stories in their life-lines
and the lines on her hands are exactly like mine
hers are three shades darker
palms trace-back the past
like mine trace-out the future
in her caress: I feel midnight
in her anger: a left hand smack
that brings back her mother's fury
my mother's fear

It isn't always easy to heal
the agony tucked in the cracks of ancestry
when slavery shackled whole parts
broken beautiful is how I see her heart

VI.

Her heart ticks like a clock
that knows timelessness is the backdoor lover
of every beginning
she gives like the beggar in Magdalene
gave to Jesus
I know her selflessness deserves a written thesis
but all I have are these poems
I hope her soul can read them

New World Order in 6

The government marries corporations
walks down the isle to kiss congress
then sends their well-armed babies
to new countries
who grow up to be masters
of enslaved nations

•

We Might Escape

Here
we are a forest of mismatched trees
immigrants, hipsters, explorers, refugees,
indentured servants, slaves, troops,
runaways, tourists, evacuees

Who's streets?

Our streets
are being sold to a system
that displaces the poorest

Here
you can die thirsty
hungry
or trying to cross their borders

Here
we've learned to steal
the very essence of life
has no where to hide

If we could
we would steal the sun
and sell it to the highest bidder
market the darkness
as a cure for the sleep deprived sinners

Here
fear has a passport
and moves freely
between the borders we invent
and the boundaries we patrol
to protect imaginary wealth
and the sweatshop gear we can afford

Here
we are surrounded
by multiplying fences
chain linked
white picket
barbed wire
electric

A people made separate
by fear and income gaps
prison walls
highways
razor wire
and train tracks

There's a gate being built
around a community
who colonized a hill top
that was once a plantation
once a ghetto
once a nation

Before the Indigenous were fenced off in reservations

There's a fortress being built
around our elevation
they've built up surveillance
around our memory's landscape

Because they are scared

We might escape
if we remember
our daydreams are ancient

They got minutemen
ready to shoot down migrating thoughts
that might lead towards liberation
or illegal imagination
of a world that exists beyond
the borders that they arm

But vision
without execution
is just a hallucination

And I grew tired of pretending
freedom was around the corner
when I never gave her my address
or invited her over
only longed for her company
without dismantling my borders

Don't be lost to forgetfulness
we are the messengers
delivering blessings in riots and psalms
we surrender to light
white flags in our palms
that wave with the breath
of our ancestors' songs

Who wrote hymns
studied stars
built pyramids
mapped the sky
sketched their hearts
nails to palms
to tell the prophecy
of now is the time
when the while buffalo rose
from the ashes of extinction
life has spelled her name
across our scars

Our words are the water
reshaping rock
our actions are sledge hammers
to apartheid blocks
our dreams are the keys
to prison guards' locks

Our consciousness a collection of awakening thoughts

That decided one day
to release all the fear   —
we were taught
and give in to love

Unfiltered
like sun to the dawn
unconditional
mother to son
unexpected
the enemy who put down his gun
against the command that hailed from above

A peace prayer
the shout of thousands of drums
the power of the people
is the power of one

Mis Ancestros Caminaban

Mis ancestros caminaban
con aire entre sus pies
cuando la niña, la pinta, y la santa maria
vinieron con su ley
teníamos el sol
enterrado en nuestras venas
pero el colonizador agarro
pintandonos de pena

Hablamos nuestra historia
con lengua despegada
el pasado con su esposa
cuya espalda fue azotada
y de su vientre generaciones
con las piernas amarradas

corriendo hacia un futuro
quienes calles están cansadas
cuando ellos de la tierra
para el cielo le empujaban
y con bala y espada
a sus hijos le mataban

Geography

The umbilical cord was cut
prematurely from my mother's land
left me between a half-learned language
and one I couldn't understand

my lungs struggling then to utter these syllables
covered in molasses
the words came out
half broken

I am the geography of a plan gone wrong
My
Amarillo
Azul
y Rojo

Mixed with this
Red
White
and Blue

leaving me shades of brown and autumn
blooming

I am the geography of my grandmother's hands
in her I find myself
stepping outside of a culture with borders
I never grasped
or made my own
never placed beneath the sown ground
my once ripe vegetation is the site of excavations
mathematically destroyed

As a child I turned in my sleep
in protest of having my mother too far
my roots cut off
my accent fading under the sound of car alarms
and ghetto mentality
TV waves
bathed in classism

In this land of the free
where children are taught to walk hard
on eggshells and backs
I was untying the unnamed revolt of my country
where children are taught the pulling of triggers

Yes, I have become one yellow wall
pissed at what my people are doing to each other
blindly carrying out foreign orders
that sometimes in my sleep
I breathe their protest with screams and fists of rage
hold bitter taste in my tongue
for their once justified cause
turned sour with years of war

yes, there are those who are running
from bullets right now
for believing in peace
while I make puppets and dance on the streets
for what I believe in

I am the geography of their father's limp body
slumped over the kitchen table
baptized in ammunition
as they walked in to find their childhood
gurgling blood from his lips
for believing in peace
while I work and pay bills

they run alongside mothers and sisters
hide out until kicked out
because one more mouth to feed
can be devastating to the system of a family
where a foreign economy thrusts itself
against the thighs of a crying country
screaming rape

When we all know it should be screaming fire
or mercy
or justice
or hold me
and love me
until my winds
are the anticipation of something beautiful
not something breaking or bursting
like bone

Shot up for a cause
that has left my mind an orphan
my body in exile
my people running
and falling

So I've become the geography of my own revolution
where every breath is a statement to be reckoned with
these hands outline those of my grandmother's
and the land she has sown

in the belief that one day
I would speak of these things
not out of fear
but out of necessity for peace

An Open Letter to christopher columbus

My ancestors rested easy under the shade of trees
roots clung to the earth like unborn children
when columbus tattooed his name on their seeds

Born of his rape
I was raised by his descendents
I carry the poison of his sword
the killing intent on leaving us drenched
in someone else's language

columbus, you dragged disease in your blankets
dreamt up demons who built your home
sand scripted your bones
the gold you longed for
left us without a home

helpless and alone
because you took it
without knowing

The sun from our fingertips
you stole it
carried it away in the corners of your smile

I was there
tasted the water you left behind in our lungs
I remember choking
on my own blood
and spit
and vomit

As you chicken-scratched your name
on my great, great grandmothers' ancestor's breast
my great grandmother's hands
her single palm could outline constellations
lines that mapped out your voyage

God?
God must have been preoccupied
turned the other way
molding Mayan songs as they lifted towards the sky
so she wouldn't lose them

You?
you were covering the distance of a pregnant earth
with one hand
savaging me with the other

Choking me

because your cousins
they kept coming

built their homes
consecutively, kept rising
thought they could
poke God's third eye

but my ancestors were all
in there watching you
murder their children
by leaving us silent

The Past

The past made our backs heavy
Feet braided
Not so steady
All along holding wings
We haven't yet tested

Take It Back

When Hip Hop was first born
I was in my mother's thoughts
not yet formed
in the womb of her intentions
half a world away in South America

It was the beat that got me
when Hip Hop was just a baby

it dropped me off in a field
when concrete was all I could feel
for miles

It was
U-N-I-T-Y
U-N-I-T-Y, that's for UNITY
that showed me back to me
when I first arrived
with no tongue to call my own

It was
Oooh child, things are gonna get easier
Oooh child, things will get brighter

That's how I got my history lessons
because when Hip Hop could barely walk
it was educating young minds
and winding the truth through capitalist clocks
who said the art wouldn't stand the test of time

mainly because they were scared
that the beat got them too
nodding their heads to stories the ghetto produced
and rich America had little to do
with the cardboard swing of things

when swinging arms became bridges
to hold bodies up
legs pointed straight towards the sky
Break Dancing was formed from broken souls
who found inside themselves the song of birds
and figured if they could sing like that
well shit, they could fly too!

Examined their bodies
to discover that bones are hollow
like drums are hollow

In time shoulder blades sprouted wings
and lower backs could bend
like big mama's voice on Sunday church could sing
spinning so fast on concrete
made the sun-dance across skies

dizzy and drunk
B-boys and B-girls would dream
locks and pops
they found the beat

Spray-painted it across their backs
traded in heavy burdens of generations passed

when Hip Hop was born
it made a waaaaaaaaaaaail
out of its mother's womb so loud
the earth felt it years later

But like my elders always told me
baby, when you strive for glory
the devil tests you
predators want a taste of you
gazelle, you better grab them legs and run
catch the horizon between your teeth
and invite the sun to rest on your tongue
because there might not be another sunrise to come

Hip Hop was doing just that
and as the music born of the Bronx
grew coordination and rose
the rich men on top found ways to change its course
so it would walk away from its source
and become a resource for their wallets
while Hip Hop's throat grew hoarse

All of a sudden HOpE lost a P
and the clanking of bling-bling
took over freedom's notes
bodies slowed down
nodding heads took up the sound
all saying yes
as jewels of truth
were being dug back into the ground

While mothers excavate diamonds
to make us feel rich
our imagination sags below waistlines
so we can't run fast
or spread our wings

Some of Africa's most beautiful
are born without limbs
because radiation machines don't discriminate
but the wealthy who own them do
and if her sons dare come to America
and fall in the mentality
their shiny bracelets would fall off
their knobby wrists too
twisting American dreams into the hands
they will never look down to see

Now this is how the world turns and skips beats
but Spirit can't dance to bullshit
so, make the beat sing
reattach umbilical chords to vocal strings
who speak the truth
ending prayers with Emmett-
Till then I want to tie ancient tongues
with Adidas shoelace strings
so it feels like something when you run

and we have to run
while spreading our wings
because bones are hollow
like drums are hollow

Diamond

Freedom from within
reshapes bone structures
so we can stand up better

Freedom from within
takes butterfly wings
and turns them into I love yous
so deep

that the echo of such words
vibrates in the hollow of one's chest
First
understands self love
First
never tries to give what it doesn't have to give
First
we have to realize
that this hate, that has kept us down
is not the hate, you will allow
to dress you up every morning

You, with your head so low
you might crash into a wall
don't let them misinterpret the best of you
has faced Goliath

You have walked away
with breath in your mouth
whether you knocked him down
maybe this time
he just walked away
next time
carry poison in your tongue
a rock in your back pocket just in case
and let him know
who David was

Because it has been too long

It has been too long
that silence has choked the best of us
us birthing the world everyday
baptizing it with milk

Don't let them cut out your tongue

What made you think that it was okay
for him to decorate your face in purple?
to cut the Oak of your body down to a seed?
don't let him cut out your tongue

Woman, speak up!

Up is the only direction
we have to go
from here on in
the ends of our unraveling threads
must be knotted up and tightened strong

Tie it around your waist
so when you feel yourself slipping back
into the black that outlined your dreams
and kept them confined
we can pull you back
into the surface where birds take flight

It is not their love
that you are looking for
it is your love
that you have lost

It is not in the structure of their castles
where you will find it
your treasure
is not the gold that they are offering

You might bandage your wounds
a thousand times, woman
watch them heal on the surface
but your birds are trapped inside
how are you supposed to take flight with them?

Head of the table never meant
he carries a spout to smack you with
unconditional love never meant
that the conditions of your survival
would be questionable

But here we sit crying
cause you were 13
when he raped you
I'm 23
and he hits me
you're 53
and it's been 23 years
that the echoes of his words
whispering: "You are worthless"
has made you into a defeated warrior

Warrior, Get Up!

Find your weapons

Whether it be your voice
or your leaving
your fist
or your dreaming

take back
what is yours

Self-Love
is not found
in an other

You are not that diamond
You are not that diamond

that children's hands excavate from African lands
to sell to American hands before our weddings
because it is the only love we can interpret

you are that diamond
that sits in the sky
so bright
only God
could have shaped it

You are that diamond
You are that diamond

I remember

I am that diamond
I am that diamond

I am
that diamond
only God
only I
could have created

When the Night is Kidnapped The Day is Ransom

When I was 15
I cut into my wrist so deep
the Red Sea
did not part
and I almost drowned in it

There was no Moses
No compass
No guide dog
No shelter from the storm

my parents were immigrants
and toilet bowl sweeping the graveyard shift
almost had their oldest carrying a shovel
to her own funeral

When I was 15
circumstance strangled my soul
until my body felt empty
so I swallowed way too many pills
to fill the spaces
desperation cracked at the edges

When I was 15
I lost the flame in my eyes
one night after too many drinks
and too many drugs
and too many
can always bend
the backbone of life

I resurrected

Before the casket closed-out years of dreaming
poetry gave me CPR
a paintbrush jumpstarted my heart
music a tourniquet to stop the flow of pain to my heart

I'm writing this poem
15 years and 15 months later

Today I saw a rainbow in a cloud
and laughed so hard
and loved so deep
and discovered that gratitude
is an open door to happiness

So I needed to write a Eulogy
for that girl
who almost died too many times
that girl who's now a woman

A woman, who loves fearlessly
because fear
is the opposite of Love
and Love is
freedom's undressed home
sheltered from the storm

Box Breaker

I don't fit into the mold they gave to me
I threw too many stones
into the glass house I use to be
shattered their assumptions
and their paper cut identity

yeah, it was me

I'm too many complexities
for their geometry
I'm concentric circles
you can't box me in

too many past lives
to get to know me
you'll have to study archeology

I'm from the outer-spaces
best master your astronomy
decode the code of ethics
till your soul guides your psychology

then step to me

take two steps back
and three steps forward
I'm somewhere in the middle
where humanity's not murdered
for technology

I started composing my apology
remembering the memory forgotten
in the deadly game of progress

they profess futures untouched
but instead regress
to women walking streets
full of fear and purses clutched
and men with guns and hidden tears
scared of a soft touch
and souls hungry for dollars
but you can't eat money for lunch

I say
dreams with broken legs
need to grab hold of a crutch
cast a new shape
from the healing that will come
until bone is strong as feathers
and can carry you through flight

Outside the walls
from up above
freedom is too beautiful
makes their box
don't look like much

yeah, it was me
I threw the stone
against their disbelief
to break my prison hold

I was too much bad kid
for their straight line
too much rebel
for their design
too much dreamer
for their demise
too much outside the dotted line
I drew my own conclusions

Pulled myself inside out
and saw that I was God
God told me:

"Yeah, it was me
I sent my only begotten son
along with all my daughters
countless poets
those who could outrun
unravel their mythology
till their formation comes undone
the only path back to me
is a step into an unknown journey
knowing you
is knowing me
when you opened the door
as I first knocked
I was a mirror
waiting for you
I guess I'm Buddhist in my heart"

wow, God
you're deep

Deeper than their churches
I guess you're just like me
we never fit inside their house
we rather walk the streets
and pump our fists in silence
with the Zapatista mass

Thanks for holding my sling shot steady
as I broke this ceiling made of glass

For All My Young Sistahs

You were born of stardust
crafted from the sun
the universe is mirrored in your tongue
so when you speak you build nations to come
and there's no way you can hold back
like night can't hold the dawn

Weaving darkness into light
you've been sharpening up your tools
cause doubt is a dull knife
fear a useless maze
that comes right back around
swallowing beginnings
before they can be found

No Room in the Shelter

She looked like a bridge
from afar

When the wind blew
she shattered by my feet
into a thousand pieces

She was a bottle flung
from the sky's ceiling
she was glass
liquored tongue
and in my lacking
I tip toed past

NYC

A sky perpetually bruised by city lights
The night and I
Can barely see each other

Past the halogen lamps
First wishes hover midway
Caught like moths to light

Yet, the first star stays virgin in the sky
Long enough to keep my faith believing

Occupation

I fell in love with you
under a sky without a moon
when you took all of my winters
unveiled summer in my womb

Freedom in your chest
in your breath I wrote a poem
and when I put my heart against yours
the birds inside you sang a song

but your wings got them jealous
they ran into our home
stole all of our children
put bullets in your throne

The birds inside your chest
flew south to get away
all singing songs
whose melancholy
crept into the dead

A victim of occupation
my soul, their calculation
not the rising sun after your death
made an impression

They stole my brown eyes
for oil pipelines
bombed all the temples
destroyed the schools
there'd be no more questions

Took my love
I not my own possession

The life you gave me
turned into deserts
inside my chest
a hollow vessel

I stumbled for days
didn't know which way to go
so I traded all my will
for a moment in your home

but your home they burned down
most ran from the sound
of a thousand raging soldiers
digging their flags into our ground

the sound of bullets
built burial mounds
where once in humans
spirits were crowned

I found their bodies on the streets
looking like shadows and fallen debris

Our silent echo carried in the wind

the trees where vacant
myself forsaken
wondering how
my world was taken

When from a distance
the last shot rang
deep within me
thunder sang

I watched the bullet exit my chest
another casualty
as if casually
my breath was theirs
to take

Memory

Sugar in my wounds
is all they left
honey bees after my death
came to heal the rest
fell in love with you first
was your child in the next
memory mapped the depth
through lifetimes
and past lives   /
weaving patterns
like snowflakes
and kites lines
in Afghanistan
in war
and past time
under fear
and blue skies
trail of tears
and disguise
to get out
of Germany
now Palestine?
Stop and Frisk
and Oscar Grant
concentration camps
and starry heights
Pinochet and desert nights
where mothers search
for bones
teeth

or any sign
of history's repeated crimes
reservations
and stolen tongues
small pox
and knotted lines
body in noose
canary bird
never came out of the mine
a sign of the times
dark bodies in chains
triangular trade
and prison lines
metal detectors
cops in classrooms
perpetuate and confine
imagination is on the decline

So I sat in the front row
to stop the flow
'cause we must re-write
history
must re-write
ourselves
until we're in it
not half-assed
or half told
or part owned
therefore sold
born of this trauma
got it from my mama
needs to be healed

from the inside
DNA tree
gotta re-root
to rewind
time travel
till we're back
capsize this ship
to downsize
need to inflate this dream
make a buoy
and still let my head get baptized
in whatever water wind fire
stargazing sunrise

Tajeme

You could hear the sound
of the steel against his body

Still

ricocheting throughout our ribcages
the day we lost him
our hearts
excavated out
left a hollow impression of life

like the 6-foot hole in the ground they put him in

Our spirits bent with the weight of his casket
the winter threatened to crack us open
like the autopsy report
and the newspaper clippings
I'm sure his mama must've cut and saved
for fear of missing him too much

We pulled from the sky
and collected tears on our collarbones

She tucked herself into the folded edges of her son's
eulogy

We all walked around like question marks for weeks
backs so round
knees threatened to buckle

It's a dangerous place
to find yourself .
angry
with no answers

with no solid ground to stand on
we were floating sage

No lights on this stage
these weren't actors
on the block they killed him
the cops laughed at us
for burning candles
and I wondered who had taken their humanity
not even hollywood could have conjured up this sickness

I wondered about the preacher
whose voice riddled bible passages
.throughout the funeral
and compared his love to the love of Jesus
but misrepresented this poet
who wrote prose for the universe's stolen moments
when he asked all the men
to either unwrap their heads
or leave God's home
with their anger still woven within them

His God doesn't have arms wide enough
for the Rastas
the Muslims
the Jews
the mourners
Tajeme's friends
who pay homage by covering their entryway to heaven

People have a million ways of disrespecting life
you don't have to pull a trigger

but somebody shot him
multiple times in the chest and arms
to payback someone's miscalculated footing

We don't know what happened

all we know is that the NYPD sees
black
male
6 feet 5 inches
Gun Violence

and I have to laugh to keep from crying
when I think of bullet prices
statistics can feel like sugar in the sun
to an already open sore

25 cents for a round of bullets?
it costs less than a penny to kill a human
a brother
an artist
a giver
a believer of life
a dreamer of the impossible
a magic maker
who grabbed your hands
and made the impractical toss-able
an open door
the Cheshire Cat's smile on a broke journey
the wind against your back
if you were hauling ass
or moving
from this side to the other side of Brooklyn

it didn't matter

his hands were big
curled into a fist his heart was bigger
a sunlight keeper

we know the stars whitewashed his soul
on his way to the Creator
and left no sign of gunpowder
or the smell of fear on his killers

A penny to a death
can cost a fortune to your spirit
and all this violence paints
is a people not worth living
in a culture that incarcerates the darkest children

My heart is bleeding
from the cold slap insult of ignorance
a post-traumatic slave syndrome
where we settle arguments
like slave keepers

Who planted these seeds?
and who's gonna reap them?

television already brain washing our self image
got us scared of looking deep
cause we're scared of the dark
and black is bad
and the depth of our soul is a black hole
that might stretch time and reinvent the unknown
from impossible to the unbelievable

so we tell white lies to our inner children

and hope the root cause of this tree
is strong enough to keep this landslide from slipping
but we're dripping more than sweat
playing the wrong hand we've been given

Even though none of us can believe it

my brother's death is not a coincidence
he is a catalyst for reconfiguring
the sacred geometry of living

Emmett Till

Living in Chicago
he was Mississippi bound
mother warned him of the vultures
"skin speaks awful loud,
never look them in the eyes
their spirits never found
you'll lose yourself searching
always keep yours to the ground"

With a kiss and hug goodbye
she slowly let him go
wouldn't if she'd known
he would never come home

In the heat of Mississippi
he whistled
smiled
maybe said thank you
maybe didn't make a sound
but the woman took offense

the white of her skin
disgusted by his face
made it a point that his life be replaced
by the outcry of a million
whose ancestor's blood
already stained this place

Sniff, sniff
the wolves were out to get him
in the middle of the night
it was his life they came to pound
out of his chest

paid no mind to uncle's screams
escaping from his mouth
as the door was pried open
body dragged into the silence of the forest
where no creature made a sound

Except the family tree
who realized that from its limbs
their baby would be lynched
surfaced from the waters
his body later found

The jury held no guilt
there wasn't enough reason
angels go to prison
and the devil was acquitted

He was 14 years of age
when his mother couldn't recognize
the shape of his face
or again hear the beauty of his song
barbed wire
car engine around his neck
like a stone
drowned in the Tallahassee
till his last breath was gone

And though his death led a revolution
fed a flood for some solutions
still the KKK is hired by the state
easy with the trigger-finger-minded

our young become the targets
with tryin' cryin' mamas
who kneel down every day
so the bounty on their children
not make them candidates for the dead

But, Michael Ellerby was 12
when he was shot down
Aquam Selman 14
when his heartbeat hit the ground
Timothy Sainsbury Killed by a rookie
on the rooftop of his house
for whistling at white ladies
who took form up in the clouds
Fruitvale station uprooted Oscar Grant
Sean Bell's 50 bullets pulled the scream
that he last sang

Thousands of souls
killed by men with awful egos
dressed in blue
serving the white eagle
guns drawn
waiting for the signal

Ignorance persistent
badges on their hearts
they're burning crosses
bullets are baptizing
giving names
to the fears they have implanted
no wrong doing
when the law's steady behind them

But

Emmett is the bullet
Emmett is the trigger
Emmett is his cousins going into prison
Emmett is no budget for proper education

Emmett is the morning when we breathe our own
salvation
Emmett is a prayer cradled in our tongues
molded from the whispers
our mothers' mothers sung

The Moon and Us

Obama won the Nobel Peace Prize
the day the U.S waged war in the moon
shot her up
looking for water

She was bleeding in outer space
every woman felt it
in her womb

They blasted a hole in her surface
because we're finally desperate enough
because the people in charge have gone mad
because something's in the water

because bombing the planet
and children
and pregnant woman
who will soon bleed again for life
is not enough

so they bombed the moon
like children cartoons
back in the 80s

•

A World Where

I want to live in a world
Where freedom is love
and love is God expressed
In every breath unexpectedly

Where forgiveness has a home
never endings come to rest in

I want to live in a world
where courage to be
courageously you
Is not all that courageous

Love is Resilience

We are hung till the noose expels our last breath
we are stoned on the streets
hammer to flesh

but the length of our love
transforms borders
like butterflies to death

Our murders are written off as break-ins
our heads kicked in
'till there's no face left
to face the shame of it

ribcages cracked
to house your fear
cause you can't excavate the pain of it

our bodies in contortion
to make space for all your hate

bound and gagged
we hold your silence

you dress our loudest voices with your violence
we hold hands in public as defiance

you say we're twisted?
we'll profess our love with skillful contrivance
you can call us blasphemous
we map our way to God
through celestial guidance

and when legs are broken
our wings unravel
to pull us from subsidence

Like Today Loves Tomorrow

I love you like forever loves never endings
like the past loves memory
like the future loves mystery
and the present loves mastery

I am a gypsy on your lips
a philosopher in your body
a vagabond in our love
I don't want shelter from

In your reflection I have grown
my ribs no longer bend inward
you turned me inside out
so I could greet myself from within

You've greeted my ghosts at your door
and in your home
you have housed them with flesh
sent them back out into the world anew

Woman, you have mended more than you have broken
stitched more than you have torn
conjured more than you have idled
gathered more than you have thrown

If I could I would grind thank yous
and fill time's hourglass
so that you could feel the infinity of my gratitude
for lifetimes to come

I have seen you rise
from the wreckage of sorrow
appear from the storm like a rainbow

I love you like today loves tomorrow
and may my tomorrows always
interweave you in their unfolding

Because you inspire me
like the power of words do
like forgiveness and never-endings
like maybes still hold possibility
and possibility no boundary
like freedom has hands
and a home with no walls

cause maybe
we can expand
beyond the confines of this world
inspire new beginnings
maybe we can be witnesses
to our own resurrection

like music to Hip Hop

you've been on my heart
like a beat to a turn-table
and your heart
is the deejay of springtime

Yes

Your love's got me blooming
like April rain brings May flowers

maybe one day
we'll name each of our daughters
our love be our sun
orbiting us

for we have orbited lifetimes
and lifetimes to come

You & I

You crashed into my stretched skin
pulled rhythms out of me
like time pulls healing from the wound

needless to say
my response came in poetry
and our conversation moved
in a slow dance
A thick prayer
with strong knees

Let Me Make Art to You

Sweet moonshine on my lips
with you inside my sacred
leaving nectar for the bees
you take me home where I was orphaned
bring me down on both my knees
so I can take a better look at where the earth begins

it's there that I've tattooed the way we love
constellations make bedding for my dreams
when you are far and flying
it's there that we shall meet

Stir the birds inside my chest
not even they would fly south
if the warmth of your love is there to breathe
the soliloquy of spring
sung to guide their migrating wings

Sweet moonshine
let me make art to you
stroke ten thousand days inside your ribs
I'll give you wild horses
reckless against your sunset hips

and still
in the stillness of darkness
I'll unearth a forest for all our doings
because I've met you
every lifetime I've ever lived

Your Heart

This place is of holiness
I remember
to take my shoes off

The Conversation of Souls

I.

The composition of you
is encoded in my being
my last name is only a disguise
gather me at your river's edge
I am there, waiting to be opened
shatter this glass container
my messenger has put me in
the script is not riddled
I am explained in simple text
and poetry

II.

Why waste so much energy
shedding tears
if the ocean collects me?

My soul intact
no matter the wreckage

My heart encased in wanting
suspended beneath the underskirt of the sky

My love for
is my love of
the two rooted in fertile soil
yet my body shivers
my eyes release the pain
of my heart's desire unfulfilled

Then I am reminded:
in the conversation of souls
circumstance is colorless

III.

It is only in the in-between state
of holding on and letting go
that chaos exists

IV.

If you are looking for reasons
you are looking for compromise
don't wade by the shore
suspended in incompletion

The body desires
wants and proclaims

The soul declares
it does not exist in linear precaution
time and worry don't hold it back

Only when the body is louder
does the soul not exist
in freedom's presence

V.

Come into yourself undone
barefoot and in reverence
you are the temple's prayer

Not even nakedness is enough
walk in without your mind,   ·
praise in your heart

Your prophecy is the conversation
between you and your spirit
reflecting truth back onto you

let you
hear your psalm

VI.

Doubt settles like dust
stir the wind
breathe life back into yourself
and shake the moment

Dress tomorrow in possibility
unraveling threads of yesterday's faltering
for today is naked
casting the longest shadow
bare she stands and looking through you
be joyful
even through the passage of fear

•

Let Your Dreams Be Your Boss

•

For the Courageous

You
who replants today despite unwelcoming soil
so tomorrow can be worthy of the roots;
Your children will grow up to be oak trees

You
who cracks lies
until the grass finds enough spine
to break concrete and taste rain
for the first time;
Your children will sing unconquered through hurricanes

You
who have named the nameless
and spoken of their suffering
so we never forget the familiarity of their essence;
Your children will be unashamed of their reflection

You
who pushes against the jagged perimeters
thrusting your weight until you can mold freedom
regardless of the danger;
Your children will dance bravely through sorrow

You
who goes barefoot and empty handed
despite the boots heavy and gun you've been given
leaving destiny untouched;
Your children will be prophets,
have fate pressed against their eyes

You
who has been brave enough to move through the
earthquakes of heart-break
and carry with permanence love into ancestry;
Your children will forgive the ghosts who have haunted
their nights
and open the door for their departure in the morning

Carve Me, Carve You

Maybe if we had carved each other
out of wood and stone
spent days and nights vigil
sculpting heartbeats, spines, and fingers

Maybe if you breathed breath into me
and I returned the favor
Carved your lover out of amber and earth
maybe if your hands were blistered from my birth
calloused feet from standing since sunrise
so precise with your detail

Maybe then faggot and nigger
wouldn't drip from your mouth like bitter salt
you would remember the taste of my chisel
sweat from my hours spent
making you the most beautiful

Maybe then you wouldn't
couldn't separate yourself from me
behind gated communities
car locks and air conditioning
your hands would recall
the infinite spiral on my fingertips

I would trace the arc of your spine with them
delicate against the contour of incompletion
and I'd spend time on you
cause it would break my heart to miss a thing
or see you lacking definition

You would remember me
I would keep you awake
unable to dream of anything other than me
unfinished in your studio
barefoot and half asleep

You would mold me out of dirt
breathe life into me
like when God from her womb
first gave birth
you would see me as your creation

Your love for me would sprout life
with no hesitation
a reflection of your soul's conversation
with the earth

I would remember you
cleaning toilets
working 3 jobs to feed your babies
I would remember
you who slept with razors to stop the memories
you who lost trust
saw mama smacked
lost a daddy
I would make you out of marble
no longer able to witness the weight of the world
breaking your back

You would remember me at the tip of your tongue
hatred could not fill that hollow space

Maybe if I made you out of crystal
cut you as precise as diamonds
you would feel as valuable as the life you just stole

Maybe if I bathed you in gold
I couldn't walk past you
hungry on the streets

Maybe if you had carved my hands
softened my feet
hollowed my drum
you couldn't have taken my tongue from me

Maybe if I had strained my back to reach your neck
to smooth out the lines
where your spine meets your head
cut emeralds in your eyes
to reflect the Amazon inside
I couldn't have built highways over you

Do you remember?
we molded each other in the dark
I slept soundly against the echo of your heart
you felt me growing
I felt you moving
you named me before you knew me
you came from my hands
I blistered your fingers

How could we forget?
start pulling triggers
against the very temple of our creation

We Grow, Despite Your Lies

In the belly of truth we always grow
like fetuses with seven months to go
or little children fed with water
whose streams no longer flow

Despite the drought
we always grow
in the belly of truth
just so you know
even if you block the sun with one hand
the moon still has your hold
dictating ocean currents
and the bleeding cycle of your mama's flow

We always grow
in the belly of truth
nutrient rich
despite depleted soil
we eat healthy portions of authenticity
we vomit up your GMO

so keep your shiny shoes and ties away from here
you've been fairly forewarned

We always grow
round like the Evil Queen's mirror
got your truth ready to blow
we have only one alliance
and that's the word that knows no hold
the shadow side of secrecy
got kidnapped by our glow

so when you don't return
don't hope to come back saying
we didn't tell you so

Transforming

I'm toiling
with the idea
that life's transforming

the alchemist's gold
was never the goal
and the emperor needs new clothing
not sold by the hands of sweatshop owners
blood soaked
sweat gained
sexually harassed
never a sick day
paid .50 cents
cost you 9.99
and call it globalization's novelty

but all debt is paid in full
this universe is balancing
the pendulum is swinging back
with all the force they pushed it with
so we're deploying arsenal
from lunch counters to hunger strikes
to help the flow of it

Emmett Till's casket is still open
in the contours of our minds
his mama's courage
carved an imprint into the collective consciousness
that "Yes we can"
and hell we have
even before Obama copped the slogan
We were transforming

Growing wings where there was only bone
cause there is nowhere left to go
these fires long been burning
bursting seeds wide open
trapped in the most hurt sectors of our hearts
if not now, will soon start uncoiling

Cause we are no longer condoning
or paying homage to your violence
we're employing the magic that wove life's fabric.
and we're draping it over the caskets of soldiers

Warriors are being born in their place
we no longer take orders
that keep our hearts hostage
I said, this rope is no longer the gate keeper's bondage

We're building ships with the privilege of this language
and unraveling their nooses for these sails
we trust the wind will guide the journey
of a thousand steps
the first is the most important turning

and we've been marching
since 1492
from G20 to G8
Selma to South Africa
Cairo to Chiapas
Seattle to Quebec
from the original Mexico displaced
through Mexico colonized and replaced
by hollywood to brainwash the human race

but we've been marching
through the stagnant fields of their imagination
reigniting the slow riot
the calm storm
truth be told
too many lies been bound and sold
from auction blocks to rock and roll
we bringing back that southern stroll

Nina Simone
was the original home
where swagger was born

we were born by the river
but never running alone
we've been marching
this life was never on loan

so they can try to sell their stolen property
patent life's codes for all your profits
deny the indigenous sovereignty
the last shall be first and the first shall be last
says the oldest prophecy

I'm time traveling
with the idea that life's unfurling
like a sunflower field
over Sean Bell's mourning
I'm unearthing the urgency
of Hiroshima's children
whose bones are still contorting
and little girls whose guns are learning
death's lullaby before the morning
and begging hands carve the air
where hunger rattles the deepest corners

The architecture of these times are dissolving
the master artist is reshaping
the landscape we've distorted

I'm soaring
with the idea that life's transforming
because it had to
we've leaped without a net
maybe we're falling

So make a wish
the universe is holding a transmitter to your heart
informing on the boundlessness of now and always
so carve the contours of your metamorphosis
and make a vessel for the overflowing

Thief

I wish this clock would stop
burglarizing time
because beautiful things are long lasting
And the best
Are never ending

About the Authors

Climbing PoeTree is the combined force of two boundary-breaking soul sisters who have sharpened their art as a tool to expose injustice, channel hope into vision, and make a better future visible, immediate, and irresistible. With roots in Colombia and Haiti, Alixa and Naima reside in Brooklyn and track footprints across the country and globe weaving together their voices to tell powerful stories that expose injustice, dissolve apathy with hope, and help heal our inner trauma so that we may begin to cope with the issues facing our communities.

Since their debut as a duo in 2003, Climbing PoeTree has organized 25 national and international tours that have taken them to hundreds of venues from Los Angeles to London, Honolulu to Havana, Chiapas to Chicago, Goa to Johannesburg. Alixa and Naima have rocked concert halls, festivals, prisons, and classrooms interweaving spoken word, hip hop, and award-winning multimedia theater; and have been honorary keynote presenters at conferences and universities nationwide. Their soul-stirring performances have been featured alongside visionaries such as Angela Davis, Alicia Keys, Erykah Badu, Amiri Baraka, Alice Walker, Cornel West, Sonia Sanchez, Vandana Shiva, Danny Glover, and The Last Poets.

Alixa and Naima are committed organizers and renowned educators who have lead workshops from state institutions like Rikers Island Prison, to prestigious academies such as Harvard and Columbia Universities. With the conviction that creativity is the antidote to destruction, Alixa and Naima's artistry is deeply rooted in movements for women's power, queer rights, Haitian solidarity, prison abolition, political education, and social, environmental, racial, and sexual justice.

www.climbingpoetree.com

About Whit Press

SUPPORT FOR THE INDEPENDENT VOICE

Whit Press is a nonprofit publishing organization dedicated to the transformational power of the written word.

Whit Press exists as an oasis to nurture and promote the rich diversity of literary work from women writers, writers from ethnic and social minorities, young writers, and first-time authors.

We also create books that use literature as a tool in support of other nonprofit organizations working toward environmental and social justice.

We are dedicated to producing beautiful books that combine outstanding literary content with design excellence.

Whit Press brings you the best of fiction, creative nonfiction, and poetry from diverse literary voices who do not have easy access to quality publication.

We publish stories of creative discovery, cultural insight, human experience, spiritual exploration, and more.

Whit Press and the Environment:

Whit Press is a member of the Green Press Initiative. We are committed to eliminating the use of paper produced with endangered forest fiber.

 Please visit our web site
www.whitpress.org
for our other titles.

Colophon

The cover title type is set in Binner Gothic, a font believed to be originally designed by George Bruce at the Bruce Type Foundry of New York, founded in 1813 and acquired by American Type Foundry in 1901. It is a freeware font and can be found in nearly all the major type libraries of today.

Additional cover and interior text is set in Helvetica Neue, a font evolving from the earlier Akzidenz Grotesk typeface (originally titled Haas-Grotesk) from around 1898 and the original 1957 Helvetica designed by Max Miedinger. With it's growing popularity in the 1960s, Linotype released a retooling called Helvetica Neue which is used here.

Interior stock is Rolland Enviro 100 Trade, 55# Cream made from 100% post-consumer recycled material by the Cascades Fine Paper Group of Canada. Cover stock is 12 point coated one side only with lay flat matt film lamination.

Book design by Tracy Lamb of Laughing Lamb Design, Jackson Hole, Wyoming. Cover images were gleaned from personal and image bank selections and based on a design by the poets themselves, Naima and Alixa of Climbing PoeTree.

 **RECYCLED** Paper made from recycled material FSC FSC® C103567 www.fsc.org

Print production by Marquis Printing, of Montmagny, Quebec, Canada. Marquis Printing is certified through the Forest Stewardship Council® (FSC®).